PRESENT TENSE

Other books by Stephen Ratcliffe

Campion: On Song (Routledge & Kegan Paul, 1981)

New York Notes (Tombouctou, 1983)

Distance (Avenue B, 1986)

Mobile/Mobile (Echo Park, 1987)

Rustic Diversions (Echo Park, 1988)

[where late the sweet] BIRDS SANG (O Books, 1989)

Sonnets (Potes & Poets, 1989)

Before Photography (THE Press, 1991)

Metalmorphosis (THE Press, 1991)

five (Slim Press, 1991)

Selected Letters (Zasterle, 1992)

spaces in the light said to be where one/ comes from (Potes & Poets, 1992)

PRIVATE (Leave Books, 1993)

SOUND/ (system) (Sun & Moon, forthcoming)

PRESENT TENSE

Stephen Ratcliffe

The Figures

1995

Cover painting by Suzanne McClelland, "Anymore," 1994, 72"x72"
Collection of A. G. Rosen. United Yarn Products. Wayne, NJ.
Courtesy Paul Kasmin Gallery, NYC.
Earlier versions of some of these poems appeared in the following:
Avec, *B City*, *Big Dream*, *Central Park*, *Conjunctions*, *First Intensity*, *Five Fingers Review*, *Generator*, *Mirage #4 Period(ical)*, *New American Writing*, *Peninsula*, and *Sulfur*. *FIVE* first appeared as a chapbook from Slim Press.
The Figures, 5 Castle Hill, Great Barrington, MA 01230
Distributed by Small Press Distribution, and by Paul Green in the U.K.

for Ashley & Oona

O N E

Pen, turn left, swallow—accent on the second or down beat
speaking of screens like a shock the scarlet under disappearing blackbird's wings,
any material malleable as water—ideally speaking
the next word will be white—

white one scans the horizon, banks of clouds on the western front, Bach
on the road which holds up long enough not to finish—
hardly a whisper, the thistle stirs—

Bill Evans played a cool jazz samba, his slogan "My life, my gas"—in context
of a book of words the side of the house needs stones,
my cough allergic to spores,
his left hand kept out of sight in a glove extended to shake mine—

the scat singer warms her throttle, the twins have a room with a narrow leak—picture squirrels
through the keyhole, a child's jacket crossing the street soaked—
outside, the light fades after six—

orange cones askew at the scene of a car pulled over the cliff higher than one could imagine
the Farallones float down stream—that was one of a dozen dreams
including daylight pines for maximum sun,
45 degrees most aesthetically pleasing a pencil the drift would hold—

come live with me and we'll play gin in the attic—after hours
the cat curled on the table,
the scared-to-death-of-thunder dog gone—

it often comes to tears when she tries to leave—another shirt, other headlights
on an early morning drive around the lagoon for breakfast,
one asking how to telephone France
when six here isn't six there, the shuttle in a loom called the boat—

alcohol the antidote to some pain she learned to cut with a knife—
lights out,
it's quite warm under the down quilt—

lost behind the mountain, the drone of a saw fells limbs—he seeded the narrative
with hundreds of botanical names, two large harpsichords
in four-part harmony, then another tenor—
the egret still amid twenty ducks, rust at the edges of the white chaise—

birds singing in the pine blind, fog banks like Pigeon Point, it could be called a watercolor afternoon,
Cool Hand Luke, *The Silver Chalice*, *Hud*—the more he looks the more blank,
blank, they took the baby away just before talking—

dredge at minus tide called Kent's Folly, how far do the holes go, Beijing?—
something about a horse! a horse! to be more accurate
the river was as big as the room
so she swapped skiffs and came back, otherwise the children couldn't have crossed—

like picking up a watch at 4:21 exactly, thinking of music
without the clock—how many times does that make the Saint Matthew Passion?—
no wonder I'm so tired, I'm burned—

lighting up a Winston, the cloud pattern was like a map of France,
the silhouette of a jet above Toulouse—meanwhile, the jet stream back where it belongs,
she doesn't want to go to the party because *"dit dit dit dah,"*
the lighter leaves signed spring—

Costa Rican monsoon so loud they couldn't hear themselves touch, she wasn't interested in him
only in herself in relation to him—in the light blue cast of two o'clock
fruit flies like apples, time flies like lightning—

mildewed shoes in the closet, you can henna my hand anytime you like—
not that I want to run away from my problems, but
coffee makes me nervous,
the hole in the ceiling hasn't been fixed—

willing to listen to whatever she had to say if swapping words were physical,
lunch less than half an orange—
three phone calls later, east winds, off-shore smoke—

Gould's *Goldberg Variations*, the wind in pine ensemble under the direction of someone—
problems develop with a dog, bay like glass, swell dropping,
red slippers under the shoe rack
like trying to decide where to stop in water—

the stone in her compass barely centered,
in the field of yellow mustard a not quite random pattern of shoes, the laundry basket piled high
as Monet's years at Giverny, Margaret's keys in the still of the night—

Lisle cotton is a lovely color, "Triste" is traditional
like "Solitude"—if you haven't seen the movie in such a tall glass
its name in Spanish sounds like a shadow
displaced proportionately to the object that casts it in pseudo-American Greek—

let's ask our master in the book, do splines make table legs joiner?—
he calls it music, she calls it sound, the basic two-four rhythm over a rollicking five-eight bass
—without these glasses I'm blind—

nor do the Yellow Pages list the awesome power of winter storms,
the straight-backed rocker no one sits in, the sand-filled piano in need of a tune,
riots in Madrid, mites in your ear, a flea on the pillow,
où sont les jeunes filles d'antan—

like Attic prose, John didn't live in his car but fed the cats there—
his hand-held left foot heard the sea better upstairs,
where whitewashed rafters seemed to recede like an upside down ship's ribs—

sixteen feet above flood stage, Robert Mitchum felt most proud of his long marriage—
"the late" meaning she was dead, left turns on left arrows only
if you don't play the same range all the time,
look when the angel smiles at you, cloud reflection racing over the water—

over greens they can't putt, bogeys by ex-Masters champs
Seve (not Steve) and Jack (spasmed back)—since he can't sleep with the lights on
the blue coat hangs in the closet—

clock reading 9:13 for six years, proceed according to logic—
he found himself lapsing into a language he didn't know, one into which others look for current
the same as I into you, moving parts in music holding together at times
as distance might collect pianos, cymbals, scat—

when people all over the world start the evening with red, what starts with "t,"
ends with "t," has "t" in it, and so on moves to the next
coincidence of certain pages—

this could be anywhere going home to breakfast—someone from California
the plant shakes, stars on the porch more than enough,
the word before the smallest of rooms
coming up the back stairs whether they'd slept together or not—

light, think of the gate whose carriage bolts are tinted blue,
a choice based on color in the first place—there are so many ways to desertification
pushing a broom around the pyramid post—

realistically, as if you knew what she wanted but now forget,
a voice in the hall asking for water—the autobiography of motion pictures
cymbidiums on an altar above the blue sea, wind
sound by continuous draft—

like whatever sudden [illegible] order, absolutely selfless
shifting to "want"—
how versatile the words non sequitur—

TWO

Whatever happened to the feeling inside
"colorful paintings,"
a literalization of its distance,
the begonia says she wants another drink—

sifting up from the lower regions of not counting sleep
where there isn't any there—in whose name I'm taking leave of Venice
"into the very water that she lights"—

just a word "string," arbor ardor—the road turns over the bridge
back to Tulsa, the olive oil can
with its quiver of pencils, idle threads of rain
in a khaki coat aboard the hovercraft from Ramsgate to Calais—

the swell came up from the west via the window
in a conversation he couldn't follow—basset hounds and voices composed for a picture
the opaque beet colors carrot red, advances in non-syntactic prose—

an eight-year-old listening to feathers in the quilt start to bunch,
the piano a narrative question of which hotel,
which head on the pillow
when the tape stops—Arthur must have shot her in his dream—

why is Madame licking the cancelled stamp—both fathers of daughters
feeling a mist on their heads as it snows rain, Pavarotti's birthplace is also a good question,
encore "Sorrento," static drowned by the ultimate O—

a line of patients dressed and undressed, the deer
at the Chinese-red front door—name the star between clouds parting,
light on the road mirrored on the ceiling, wind
sounds in grass and tree—

as soon as she turns off the light falls asleep—wild bees in a column,
where the grass was cut mounds,
the full moon drives him to the edge of crazy—

X counts Y and Z friends, hard contacts—in a jacket zipped to the chin,
his child grows up to shoot the president
but cannot tell what feeling he had or what they called
disordered thinking—Thoreau was right about the lives of desperate men—

first she was in Florence, then the alarm went off—
the fire chief's wife didn't believe the house was burning, a three-minute song
like "He's so fine" is over so soon—

before the cancellation of the summit, newspapers reported bombs going off all across the Alps—
details like the preceding one suggesting how voices repeat the syllables
"license blue," "dust breath," "redwood drills quick,"
play like Rosewall, paint like Cézanne, the pencil probably lost for good—

how suddenly one becomes ten—the dog shouldn't walk on his bandaged foot
but stand on it more or less less than before,
"I love the way she talks like Ellery Queen on the table"—

the *pick*, *pack*, *pock* of balls splashing in a bowl of air, peonies
the butterfly flew or ripped from,
wistaria espaliered past flower—"a smell of roast fills the air,"
Drummond of Hawthorndon said to Ben Jonson, who replied "why not in the car as elsewhere?"—

after shocks rock falls, coffee fatigue,
the smelt caught in a gull's talon—the weathered wood drinks up paint,
the other a shower in tile-green enamelled blue jeans—

ironic as boring work in a beautiful garden, Catullus
loses his temper at dinner—springwater jars
filled at the tap, the pergola waits
until the bees leave, de Kooning asleep on the fridge—

my father raised in Tulsa suggests the cigarettes on the desk she doesn't smoke,
autobiography a fiction that covers the scraps on which I address
the photographer on the beach who shoots the sun—

the beekeeper who couldn't find his words,
hadn't worked a day in his life
so to speak, the poetry of particular matters on the table
the bright Mercedes missed—there are so many colors in the world the blind don't see—

red dogs in the morning, the motion picture stars war—she knew what a drink would do
and wanted one, nor was it absurd to stop there,
the piano to airy thinness trilling "I could feel my heart flip"—

up tempo after the drums, what does the Guide Michelin mean by "toque"—
twenty years later the same song played again,
imaginary intersect
full speed ahead read like a warning sign, NO PARKING—

when Kafka gets hard, white paint everywhere but in the news
as much like a bird as a piccolo can be—revised,
last year the SPCA spayed a million homeless "pets"—

D Minor a frame to hang Dante in true to some simple notion of self,
there isn't a time the whole world isn't out there,
which isn't as good as Whistler
but segues to something I've been thinking about Mrs. Plato—

his daughter calls him "daddy" with an *e* as in French, "*beau*"—
when she reads it's like drinking wine, "you'll ride this roller coaster till you're not afraid,"
"wire jaw shut until departure"—

one plays the music as noted, like catching thought on the wing
or the artificial stars in a Muybridge photo,
an orchestra live on the lawn
better than speaking of "her luggage went to Frankfurt"—

birds up before first light even if she isn't awake—
one of Bach's many sons wrote this—bee legs caked with yellow dust,
smell the honey on Jagger's prick—

the vestige of a tail hidden in his coccyx, Darth Vadar didn't like large crowds—
she too keeps the standard, eating steak to feed the baby
who will mow the hills tomorrow,
all of us almost sound asleep, all the paintings about to see—

did the fire come on without warning?—once, when the spider climbed its thread
Sappho was pregnant, once the reason Virgil was punk
whiskey still, lens contact—

leaving home because she didn't like to work, Nancy Smith Drew's *noblesse oblige*
teaches her the danger of long nails—after Ned Nickerson,
modest as he can be, the thing she loves best is *déjeuner sûr l'herbe*,
"nowhere to run, nowhere to hide, why must I be a scarlet tanager in love?"—

Stravinsky famous at thirty, Zappa's interest lies
in the digital recording of his cello triple concerto—to speak of the alternatives
life kills point blank—

refracted egret shadow lagoon glass—something about dense sound,
the origin of speech as it enters the work, speed
because things happen fast—
daughter a mother walks to the ocean whose job is to see, feel, hear more—

to be the green shirt blue with yellow glasses,
again the dredge called Kent's Folly—
pollens because the now mown grass, violent sneezes—

THREE

His temperature flared with violent sneezes, he was getting O
such cold feet—who was recording technology,
why was she talking to herself
in a plastic visor, was the whole box maps and books?—

like a psychic who knows the boat won't sail, ivy leaves
through the deck's cracks—a holographic codicil may be the casual term for it,
the sound of water being such a constant—

after shaving space,
Bill Evans dead at Montreux, sled the piano back upstairs—we too dream clasped together,
you take care of the baby—assuming they came from the florist
these poppies must be Mission Bells—

at crazy eights in the kitchen, Barbie consistently beat Ken—
after the massage he felt sound asleep, practically
speaking—eyelids, under neck, burned—

when the first cowboy threw his leg over the saddle
he landed on a mustang—what creates rust
perhaps the wrong word, *Taulk*
on the ancient map become the silver screen—

in the complete privacy of a toilet his hands and face only were not tattooed—
three flights up the round staircase, the cold windows
out the cold, the leg in the door who wants to shave again soon—

one reading for years the letter, grasping the moment what it must have been he said,
another pouring milk white as a kerchief, views of the house
across stippled water, diagonal streets—
was the map the clue, canal drifting south sans vent?—

sand turned under stones, building put by pieces in a box
—film, can you tell?—eggshell in yolk congealed
on the white plate in a bookcase, the mail sent down steep steps—

close strokes abstracted, the flash lit two mouths
inscribed in water still around the edges moving—when blue the seabird screams
the white beyond less line, or say the house is random
peonies reading on the table—

flavor circles the subject just as the mind clears a new mote—tense coincidentally imperfect
can't have commas both ways at once, painting frames in the film
like garden sculptures beat in a green rain—

in words that mimic the blank page dropped from the bridge
one falls to pieces walking in a park—sunglasses
sitting down to peel an apple in a field bathed in light, was she high strung
or just up tight when she handed him the second cappuccino?—

no mention of children under the bridge, someone who climbs the fence in a jacket
reminding you of James Dean—it's quiet but the air isn't fresh
down the well, who said security is a myth—

when the man without teeth requests you for supper you want to escape,
a technique by which the window opens without a sound,
water trembling on the edge of each leaf
suggesting the space one misses under someone else's door—

Eros with wings and arrows, because this was again the court, two lovers rising on a curtain of air
the current works to billow up—ground painted blue for spectacle, age has cracked
her eggshell face, the surface flat because content not form counts—

undercut slows the ball, topspin hops it—too finely tuned
to play "Besame Mucho" without discrimination, Willie the Lion Smith
stands in the sun against her bronze crotch, the taste
of pouring down the home stretch—

cool of stone walls, decorative moats, pyramidal hedges with persistent leaves—
"either this feeling is a cold or hay fever"
she said, the air through the window drafting her to sleep—

lined up topless for an English education, but why wear wool in June—
her hair floats from the balcony closing the shutters,
seconds later the siren's Doppler Shift,
leather soles on asphalt, Bogart blaring *"Hello? Harry, hello?"*—

Balzac's story becomes the stage, shapes turned
under the shadow of Pavarotti's barbed voice—so little action means to see much,
the bronze on the mantelpiece breathing deeply, *"shhhhh"*—

in the middle of nowhere Marley-le-Roi, child on her family's wavelength
loving how she smoked the Philip Morris—to quote
"finesse" unquote infinitive,
how were the scratches on her legs imagined by the people two stories down—

War and Peace vs. *Swann's Way*, Antoine and Ginette start down the street
followed by huge booms—after a while the noise takes over,
the bronze green railing framing real people—

the man in a pinstriped suit reads *The Man Called Thursday*,
Chinese reads down—smoking between courses
to clear the palate, the books to be arranged like a house
whatever order its words, *hypocrite lectrice, ma semblable, ma soeur*—

cocaine delivery to the embassy, it was the little ecstasies he counted
in the echo of voices phoning long distance—
ailing diva, neon fix, keyboard with "a" where "q" was—

Teagarden still knows how to swing
who wanted to smoke forever, slides of his travels lining the closet
proof there is more to Paris than dolls in the window of a sweatshop thrown together in a car—
tonight feels cooler, my feet are cold—

labia pinched in tight jeans, do women give men the eye men give women?—I'm in your bed
because you're on the couch, the comic meaning it's time to eat
when you know by his knife he can't—

world a garden as the master paints it, light rippling the surface
the grass boat drifts on—even under her parasol
once upon a time on such a bench
composed with yellow rake, such labor to keep off the lawn—

the crème de menthe smell of her breath, parrot on his perch surveying traffic,
table loosened after wine—turn down the bed cover to cover,
"m" as in mnemonic, "t" as in Tchelitchew—

that's how the scene looks in light, the town having left its children
a bullet the gardener aims to make chromatically correct—
chalk bluffs above the ruined bridge, February
warming his feet by the fire, in June the field in a hat, mowing—

keeping back age with broth and drugs as mortar squares the floor's alternative states,
the knife gone red an impossible-to-maintain regime—
no names recalled, they soon forgot what skinned alive was to bear—

A under C going line-of-sight to pitch until done, the mob
marches in a passage between heat waves above the walk's weedless gravel
and the starved hounds' monster bark—necks the last to go, a sax duet by one mouth interspersed
by shouts comma savage music, brass curves blowing bass momentum—

Max Ernst considered the fountain a total occasion, exit plié—
as for the fly trapped down June's neck, when the macaroon starts to sing in her mouth
she will think "patience" on the wall lit opposite the kitchen window—

FOUR

Interrupted by music, the man in the dungeon doesn't understand a thing—
he used to think a Dalmatian loves its spots,
lots of blank sits
which lead to where a singing bird exits both ways at once—

bugs and currants in a basket, the plate reduced to pits,
stones, skins and bones—one child plays home, the focus on his pistol aimed at the lens,
the other given to square-stemmed mint, silver mugs, the right bourbon—

"I once was a postcard, now am found" returning from the edge of private language,
the amber ashtray void of butts, the bottle of milk
oddly weighted, blue
lost under the lion's roar, the bedroom private as paper-thin walls—

excuse me, do the sheep go too?—read "come" and "go" in terms of breed lines
said the man with a bashed-in nose, infinitely complex
at every curve's shell, "madame" as opposed to "mademoiselle"—

bags under eyes and perfumed to procure a mucous mouth, Jane
married a great rug-wrecking Pyrenees—love's gesture gave them a child,
fffffttt when the sickle mowed them down, welcome
to an English-speaking church—

green nubs the vine, mushrooms the dripping wall
in French that's harder to speak than hear—will she or not take the train
if aspirin for an excess-caused headache has rarely worked?—

alone, having lost his shirt at solitaire,
petals of gilded wheat, electric lanterns the little ones kind of twist
to the same scotch broom Bill swept the family closet with—
after the picnic a thrush or something moves in—

another amusement was Billy's walking pneumonia
—the waitress could be the busboy's twin, her father had sex with her mother
only by appointment, though graph paper also works for addition—

two point four to the Cascade Garden
where little Tan Tan chews a hole in your best pants—
many calls later still no train, no one certain as to what this means,
grammar a means of making ends meet—

think how real cows' milk tastes, then drink down to the word Pepsi—
one grandmother in heaven, the other in Oakland,
trout in the stream nosing up—

another coffin of twigs and scraps, quaking aspen on luscious slopes
ask the thermals about the house on the left of the lawn
under clouds the paper called rain—how comic
the art of falling rock signs, how fanned the wind down steep vales—

she wakes up early not knowing why her suitcase
sprawls on the floor—but who says a president never says "never,"
the street as promised quiet after dark—

in dark glasses armed for work, the surgeon like a journal of white paint—
whose fault was it she mounted the stairs
the series repeats, child rolling down the canvas yawning
at least among friends Saturday night, a favorable gust of wind out the door—

she dreams a palette, overhead smash! foghorns sounding the distance
under foot, jackhammers like the dentist drilling her tooth,
hair in soup, moped ringing the end of round one—

mosquito at pond's surface, but why does she want to write it down?—
couldn't she just remember the possibilities were endless,
crayons attempting to catch the light's façade,
another speaking slowly to her taste?—

going to the chapel in the shade of the trumpet vine
he opens a window on giant bees, a suitcase for their many racquets,
hundreds of thousands of peaches bruised—

after hours on the road, Cézanne's mountain rearing into view,
you can tell it's her child by the way she's beating it,
how he ignores it—when he woke up Sunday and she asked do you want it
and he said he didn't want it and she said you've got to have it it was a huge grammatical eros—

the more you tell a woman how beautiful she becomes—low-voiced sound
along the Great Wall viewed as China, the Alps in aerial series above
down on her forearm, will Barbie Laurie send for Cindy Lou?—

talk about mothers, how could she die—I haven't yet begun to research times past
but used mats were called "floaters," her cigarettes and crème came
in the same blue box—meanwhile, solemn as rococco
doves, a triangle of sweat stuccos the base of Der Blau Reiter's back—

does that mean foreign policy was an aphrodisiac?—with sand for rent in the human zoo
Yves St. Laurent does not pay for the exercise of astronomy
changed to "Guano!" period—

more light she wants to work, words perfectly solid but waiting
in an exercise of lines, the sign for high winds
blowing like a poem by the bridge where Princess Grace,
falling asleep, crashed—who was in charge of the music, Otis Redding?—

swallows descending at evening, the shock waiting to be read when he opens the letter
almost like rooms at home—view from the desk of the door
to white spaces, the man in oil by himself at the window with a book—

ear to the grass, he hears himself thinking of holes in the table,
a collaboration of dogs asleep in the shade of the bank,
the turtle under leaves a multi-colored stone,
the diagonal pattern in the floor squared, the region found in its bottle—

Romeo eyes the bird on the wall—O giant purplish thistle,
does lifting his shoulder collapse
his lung? did Buddy barely hear The Crickets?—

in the absence of datelines his mind wanders from the edge of her mouth to the pillow—
to one who forgets the hand holds the pen bites mean affection,
the Eskimo ritual abduction of a bride
who tells her mother a flat lie, vertigo descending the stairs to utter calm—

"forerun faire love, strewing her way with flowers"—like Niels Bohr inventing tables,
there was nothing erotic in the way her strap fell in his eyes,
the leaf only covering Eve's patch—

stop when you read "in the middle of the road I found my life in the dark,"
two-lane traffic suicidal, the body beside the Vespa
probably at fault—one writes
a ticket, the other points his gun to where Urbino's nose becomes a window—

let X be the movie of clouds on the sun, slow motion—
O sounds as lovers take to the bedroom, an absence of windows no concern
letting your tongue bounce off the roof of your mouth—

why did he sit in front of the painted bird watching the spider
speaking to animals and Saracens alike?—
yes it's the moon
but perhaps tomorrow, was there someone before Lucia?—

strong drugs each morning, she didn't fall asleep all week—
"was moving their bags to the hall a hint?" she asked the SAVE THE CATS couple,
both of whom look like stray cats—

FIVE

The way half-thought becomes androgynous—how laughter from an upstairs window
frames the announced-to-one listening forward to the word brought
to where she slept, whose effect mirrors her lips
and tossed hair, showers she couldn't have known of, the gale in a glass of white wine—

a street by the next bridge, trenches and ranges depending on the drift
of mail boxes, the colored pencils on the stone floor lightening
like stars—legs or arms or upstairs biting without ceremony into the next piece—

running the small cat up the fence,
its eyes lit by headlights' yellow—"bowl" she said, not "goal"—
"my land's over there" he said, pointing to rows arranged in a huge sculpture park
followed by signs attention, Radio One, solid gold—

oak leaves the window screen prints with abandon, how do you plan to recycle space?—
I for one mean to view the mean Madonna no matter how long her nails, shadows under her weight
arriving without the car, by sundown shades of this ridge and that—

nothing is signed but the holes say this frame is wood—wine, smoke, carriage, camera
flash not permitted, though it's beautiful waiting to be told what to do,
who can it be now lighting the Aurora after the gunshot's
chilly echo, the host who bars the door—

other webs where the late sun lights the transom, scorpion under glass dismembered for words,
quartz planes clean as cut—you say basil, I say after one storm
the whole Sahara will be green—

think of the film of the woman making a film—
her first caresses were savage, replies simply to a question of fog
which sounds like music
voices could wound, overtone scales a trick as to cushion the bone—

white on the line that sheets his eye, how in the world did the arch get built?—
did semaphore cost as much as a lamp, that looking
in a glass as if she'd cringe impossible if the elbow jolts the hand?—

heading into the crossword puzzle, my offspring at one end of the table
something like "cork," "black wire," "cure for a seizure"
once the road narrows to one lane,
the others who will learn to drive since they can't swim—

armed with books for dinner, he grabs a knife and orders the first course—
if only she had seen his muscles chewing along the grain
but everyone was tired on the Emerald Coast, and over such a landscape who presides?—

too hot to sleep, too tired not to, she palms him slap! with the heart of her hand—
forget about the sisters who don't tell girls the basics, the parakeet
against the flower smashed, an impossible thought
leaving a scar like the smell of his pipe, which sometimes indicates spinal—

look again when the light switches on, the only Crucifix is plastic—where is the question
a retired couple kind of swings, two stray cats in the low beams
a dynamics of two or three reduced to flinging a towel against the far wall—

on an island the fire had scorched for miles she wakes up tired, why?—
the man seemed friendly enough, his arm around her waist could be love, but who *was* Sylvia
asks a voice she can't follow, others believing the way light strikes film
is a little cross which supposedly means something—

next to the church a field of dead cars desolate as ranchland California, circa 1846—
when the girls kicked up their heels in the shade, rounded shoulders even if the lights were low,
watermelon the red one, goats like a herd of Buddhists clanging bells—

lost in contemplation reading Proust, "folding pages
the rippled effect of wind in hills' green, pool's blue" are some of the words they haven't learned—
and while the Separatists want the Americans out it could blow just as hard tomorrow,
the baby's manner of background noise neither friendly nor excessively shy—

who shot Trotsky and why was he in Mexico with a dog?—
something *is* creeping into the language the Duke ran into the mirror,
"I'll lend you my mother's sequined dress"—

Sugar was her maiden name, this text in fine print so loud you can't think
the day she conceived you locking your mother out of the room,
Lydia passed out—Oscar alone felt rusty at night,
so tired of the Old South he drove his mule to the train—

unless the bed fits into such a space
pine grains until knots,
how does a doctor say her husband has the clap?—

he could have slept if he hadn't been awakened by the spine coming off the book—
a moral instinct not to return the stolen cash,
the roof still missing the tree, the pencil in hand not a view,
the thrill of Mecca a pilgrim feels on his prayer rug, directly dialing Allah—

just in off the plane from Quaalude she keeps her baby in her pocket, "religiously"
likes Roquefort, red pants, a ballerina's poses, Nikon's license to shoot the food of future worms—
please leave it in the wastebasket, or hang out till you sleep it off—

in leather sweeping the walks at four, discontinuous stops
after the parking lot where the cats spat leaving the island caged for slaughter—
no one wants to listen less than an eye gestures the wind, whose face in my lap looks sound asleep,
semi-breves, minims, crotchets, quavers, cards about to embark—

to give you my name is surely no more than familiar, like someone reaching for a ceiling fan
who just stops—having a baby is unique in the sense
interior mode, someone blaming anyone but herself for missing the book—

sunflower heads bent yellow under the sun, traffic joining the cicada
whose message reads "the only thing open was the bar"—
X lights another match, her age registered
as lines about the mouth cold as the way they didn't embrace, but why wait up or drift?—

despite Cinderella's crest-fallen foot, every shoe she liked she bought—the sky clouds think
stretching a banner over the town, her problem in eating the melon
fumbling at the keyhole in the dark—

amber fields, omnivorous polyps, invertebrate marine, the nun's black bag—
it's a drag waiting around for the next move, roof lichen, façade wrapped in a green mesh
strung across the kitchen wall above blinds,
cards, smoke, the stairwell under the TV missing the stoop—

somnambulating into maybe the wrong room, the story of feeling lost in the book—
not a right angle left in stones, floors the water boarded over,
the eyes could be anyone's but must be you—

moss on steps the water harbors, as glass cooled too fast will break,
see how many ways there are to say mother, mama, madre, mutter, mere, mare, sea—
have I gone too far to get back to glass, the tree crickets preferred
among decoys in a film, charcoal eyes on paper—

thinking of breakfast across the alley troubles my sleep
which leads to the above-implied boat, a mnemonic device for learning nines—
we know this because after work the cook slumps down with a book entitled *Return from Dachau*—

buoyed up like an old hull the waves hunger after,
Marino Marini, William Williams and Ford Ford at Restaurant Catullus,
of which nothing need be said—the oleander's poisonous pinks
are passive, but with floors like these who needs walls, I'll take the bed by the door—

piano full as when a chord stops, his hand fell asleep holding *Anna Karenina*—welcome to Mont Blanc
whose weather zones require a guide, swatches of trees meaning avalanche
signed, "I-sense-the-cherries-in-the-glacier"—

SIX

If you lower your head the cabin won't fall, "them dry bones"
a coincidence of words spelled in that order—
I hate what coffee does to me too
reading the notes weaned from my foot, the slate river pencils the torrent—

an impossible-to-decipher card, the escape to the south lined with treacle—
lean in the lung, red in the tooth, the goat on the peak,
massive white faces thinned blue—

cartons of blue smoke camouflaged in granite, look for "red"
eight or nine verbs later, the language of animals meaning *camouflaged in granite*
as one wears glasses to eat the white fromage,
then drinks a toast to the other, herself on the edge of frail—

grandfather closing the stream from whose depths wound a mill of roses, future of "sang,"
to whomever runs I am asleep—watching him eat my torture, words become
waiting for scraps beneath a moon round as it was a month ago—

scribes, limners and seal engravers worked in this crypt, producing books on regionalism
whose pages haven't yet been cut—the cat on the blue Delux
has twenty-four friends, fierce
as the way she feeds her dog filet mignon from an ashtray—

where my plate meets the dirt, little suggestions—
were they identical or mother-daughter twins, did the assassin
miss the apparently wrong guy?—

rain again an abundant source, figures at rest by the stream
mouths closed, a disaster Proust would die of
in a taxi avoiding the police,
curb water, traffic drone, deer's tongue more bitter by far than Campari—

the pipe in Shakespeare's mouth since ten
discovers the smell of coffee in his soul—what an irony to wind up
a throw from here, Millet more than food for thought—

she wasn't allowed in the room when her mother was dying,
her father stayed away hunting all the next day—other leaves in wind
like planning what shirt to wear, the dwarf at the court of whomever first is married,
dogs on blankets wounded as ever, 9:28 exactly—

hours later an hour and a half, excitement in the film sometimes
more than the film itself, which isn't answered in the scene called *Les Fleurs du Mal*,
cloudy over lake's detail, clutching my hand—

blood on her dress dark blue, dark green, dark red—
this was an I-can't-get-to-the-beach-the-tide's-up syndrome
—consumptive, amphetamines, gone
regardless of the heavy-lidded wave about to break—

carried asleep upstairs to Le Mura, a coincidence
to say the word until its substance can't be paraphrased, "eucalyptus,"
the bay one never saw so well, the wagon harder to tip over—

composing letters to himself at the end of August—so much for the image,
picture the rabbit like a silence on the table,
pencils colored in a book
by Federico de Montefeltro, "These Were All The Same"—

lately the music more intense, the color of postcards like an infant
dissolved in tears who won't eat—think of the case of an old violin, Vivaldi's
shop in the building next door, the boy on his way to unbox the instrument no one called for—

in the glare off the skylight the text "waiting for the knife, the figs, the mango"
—now you know why they don't make French windows,
the oldest cat lost in missing glass
in weather like this Jimmy Rowles, my buddy, welcome back—

oddly enough, the hardware store speaks French—his ailing prostate described
pulling barbed wire—the milkman can't finish his story,
whoever carries the gun will shoot—

saved from a bloody head by her almond eyes, he finds it harder to notice curves in the road
after a marathon, gladioli in a state of canary yellow shock, thought
flown to heaven—such is the edge among tempi,
a technique by which analysts change bees to the blossom—

Bach's flute like birdsong, partita light through fog, Martha's five degrees of vision
were good for things like cards—I opened the door slowly,
not knowing my next step, Bogart in *Deadline* in a tavern down the road—

during the hottest part of the day the fog draws in,
will you take me as far on drugs as possible?—this was an exhausted
after-lunch question, cigarettes in the ashtray, smoke
spent, piano in the breathing room—

look at the house as lonely hours in the world
of Carson City—waking to the sound of surf in the foreground, geography
like a game of maps, first name Schooner, Odessa—

periodically thinking of ways to say "A,"
"be calm," "see the whole picture"—the cops pulling up would chill your spine too,
Mount Tam clouded as Mont Blanc, buoys tilted toward tide's ebb
snapshot, meaning indefinition is in print—

this machine will answer but not record
jet storms dead ahead,
lines cut from Zambia to Zaire, the car on a ladder to nowhere—

"silhouette, silhouette, silhouette, silhouette, silhouette, silhouette"—
one could go on but it's so much later than we think,
i.e., oak leaves under bare feet,
American English most easily learned in a picture window—

ninety-five degrees in Venice Beach the day he came upon Vermeer,
Girl With Earring—the bear smiling in the lavender garden,
was this truly the color of dusk or another spider who spins its web into words?—

it's nice of course to be here, but now I'd like to show you the rooms of my house—
the painted fruit in a bowl by Diego Rivera, the box containing my collection of Bobby & the Midnights
which doesn't exist, things that don't seem to change
like the bride propped in bed with pillows, but this too is nostalgia—

for stolen keys try thorazine, for steel too hot to handle gloves—
my secret of the year is my teacher
Montagliari, Rexroth's wrath fondly remembered as dislocate personality, a sprained thumb—

assume the year dies at dawn, E-flat in the left hand
until the sentence becomes each day
like a family—when my sister-in-law asks what kind of house I live in
the phone goes dead, the screen door flies can't storm—

give the night-blooming Cereus my love, I'm going to bed—witness how the dog starts
both feet on the peddles, tilting the rectangular frame taking photos
of his father taking photos of his name on the sign—

on the domestic front, when it comes to taking orders
only a zealot would count 7, 8, 10 a run—
plumb, level and square
phone calls back and forth note the rice was turned down, probably 1850—

startled eyes through a doorway half as much as holding hands
—tape two records the playful funk in bars and clubs,
"Kiss Me Much," real Monk on Blue Note—

SEVEN

A flash of red before the turbulence strikes, Audubon says it's a Clark's nuthatch—
now pretend you're on the left side of the score, autobiographically
speaking, the text a mosquito behind your left knee
reading "impatient, don't think, paint what you feel about Soutine"—

voice through the door on a talking binge, rust-sided bugs packed to the brim—
—dream on, hit hard, change directions,
monarch with redder shoulder catching the spider's sting—

confusion of *m* with *n* isn't easily nemded—a bird chirps on one hand
before dawn, on the other wiper blades don't sound
forest green when I blink, when she takes my hand letting slowly go,
architectural script learned as a series of strokes extending to second nature ad infinitum—

tell me which mint spearmint is, noon so hot the pinecones crack
the needle-white trout's teeth bared above the coals, "an if or as to in so be it"—
gymnastics too is dangerous under the step built by X—

this story points out what miners through the ages have known, *Andra moi enepé Musa*
twirling a pencil in the shadow of the hexagonal copper lamp—
he hardly noticed Battista Sforza's smile
or the cat's head hidden behind a yellow rose, the towel wet on the spread—

they moved from New York to forget such weather, the penultimate bloom a monarch lights on
below tropical grey clouds, Manuel—
take the words "tactile dome," "periodic coughs," "thrown clay"—

squawks in the nest the still-warm egg, giving to each letter élan vital—
her inability to perform even the simplest of percentages
resulted in a settlement for the loss of an eye,
this line of questioning called embryonic, compulsive, flashlight blank—

codeine after vodka giving his headache a chance to relax,
the builder rounds the corner nailing the wall—
spell as you say the words "archipelago," "peninsula," "Chlortrimeton"—

after "home of the brave" the furniture arranged around the empty room
represents auxiliary views of the house in oblique planes—
it takes years at least to letter with finesse
voices in Spanish, flames fanned by the juice of garlic-flavored chops an alternative to sport—

cutting out coffee calmed the nerve at the end of his mind, like tropism turning pages
—Paris, Kansas, Paradise Alley—who knows whether he heard
the music of the spheres or Fats Domino's "Yes It's Me" played twice today—

the polite plot like a trauma one could live without, his swollen and bruised-looking neck
seemed to juxtapose still life with a landscape viewed as if in fact it were so—
take the cartographer who tries to posit all sides of a question
from a point termed the "third angle," posts in place of blocks, graphite meaning bass—

the attempted suicide's MBA got him as far as a floor job at Woolworth's—
at the same time, 47 percent of expectant mothers actually do
Y and Z, instances of someone honest enough to get shot in the face—

copies of the book are sometimes made available for as low as breakfast or lunch,
a case of time left at the right place as much as serendipity—
that was our East Africa correspondent
during his commute, when *two* stations neglected to report the weather—

once a blued stovepipe rusts, other aggregates
include the difference between lightning and the lightning bug—
rain here called simply a mist—

ONLY D ARE E equal to ALL E ARE D, something "artwise" from the studio arrives
unexpectedly drunk on negronis—tossing buckshot into his plate
when told his father had married a woman
of a different ilk, Lawrence replied "Dove bones for the birds, I mean cats"—

dusk bird's erratic swoops, the blow by blow account of a house not square—
nor is she squeamish pounding her left into "The Drunken Sailor,"
vertical planes extending into parodies of useful space—

as an index of output imagine K. 338, the soundscape outside Adelaide frogs—
the thing about railroads is security, a condition
the insomniac cannot forget—who could say what it signals,
just as when the French left Hanoi they took everything, even their dead—

appropriate to music in any such event, the midpoint of your life
looks both forward and back—
if Tina Turner was born in Brownsville, Texas in November 1938, what difference does the day make?—

the slide of a man spilling water from a jar was only a speck of sleep in Vanessa's eye—
southern skies instead of a celluloid candidate, multiple warheads
most of all from the moral point of view, innovation
alone blind as the last word in sunflower yellow, summercream blue—

slammed for taking a minor across the east St. Louis line, Chuck Berry bounces back with Nadine!—
saying for instance "What can you do for me now when you should've stayed home,"
my present legal difficulties going nowhere, London burning up—

a four-note mobile under the church dome's glare,
he fidgets with the doorjamb weather shut, like once when a boy dressed in a man's suit
surprised a little by his own strength, hazelnut cookies with a bit of what?—
she does the flowers, practically trilling songs of the fourth world—

two women wrapped in blankets circle the losing pitcher
who hasn't even given up a hit—confident they will soon get well, the automakers
speaking of nuclear bombs puts everything in perspective—

calling the bride to clench her flowers overhead, who would have thought the world is a glance
faces could register growing out of sleeves, rain that lets a system hold—
what finesse to say too little, let alone stop
her hand behind the curtain as it fades to a brightly-colored bouquet in the window well—

"Rag Mama Rag" on the flip side of the checkered single, a better word
would be powder—lucky she wasn't on the freeway
so angry her freckles turned red—

mushrooms this morning where just one was, after so many gavottes
the music returns to a flute—in my eye my thoughts fuse,
chlorophyll apparent in the false color image on the opposite page,
The Notebook of Malte Laurids Brigge if you can't read German costs only a dime—

how modest she was getting dressed in the Tow Away Zone!—
twice already she had gone to the castle
in the classics of tomorrow, the Cat Burglar at last caught napping on the roof—

"you'll have to finish that now or give it to me," she thinks
as soon as the train whistles, the walnut falls, the planet changes like the blue in "roof"
that lures one to Rhode Island—Argon one of the two noblest gasses,
the woodwind quintet will knock your ears off—

he liked to think of it as sound sculpture, as one continuous wall would inspire "feeling"
in the blond's reply, traffic coming through the door
in reports like this tripled in a book called M-I-S-S-I-S-S-I-P-P-I—

the wind that blows the storm back to LA seems to echo "Ce Soir à Tunise"
but such decor is "classical"—Giotto, Beatu, Piero, Vermeer,
will Dorothy return to Kansas bearing Toto,
her unhappiness extreme over the pear on the plate she thought was fake?—

as gradients and large-scale patterns vary, two huge circular cells a little like ping pong,
lots like wind—magnetic fields perturbed around the nail
T5, T6, spin, spin echo, spin—

EIGHT

To hear the music, paint the clouds "when stars begin to fall"—
speaking of the future, plant corn with a stick
in twelve tones on a mountain
when the President leaves himself what he calls "wiggle room"—

the doors were all numbered an extra hour
of time that wasn't broken—was she the reason he lost his job,
a hardy mix of fescue with perennial rye?—

going down the road he thought
to the house on the corner with the maintenance-free lawn,
the postman slips the letter through the slot—this has been a Dolby calibration tone,
music for the first 127 intervals subtitled harmonic series—

around the corner the cat suns, the blue bowl on either side of the fox or carved dog—
the bars on the bus meaning prisoners,
chardonnay's complex nose reminiscent of apples and pears—

given the parameters of sea, land, ice, soil and vegetative impact,
a reward for the rottweiler who answers to Roxie—
code words standing for real words,
this tangent indicates an attitude best described as non-committal—

despite everything she confessed with a country twang—ce n'est pas un problème
falling to the blanket on the ground the medics tended,
otherwise hushed tones—

consider the value of mauve and green to the driver who hasn't smoked for weeks—
the lady walks through the picture to a ladder on the canal
where boats can tie up, coincidentally
the barber in Hairfax, Seville who lops off frame after frame—

fog lifting fast, sunny and warm, the crane standing stone statue still—
in this frame of mind you can see why 1951 was a trap,
why "that" clauses stay in the trunk—

among continents division hardened year by year—
even in Chicago the hope remained that one could visit Sarajevo
if nothing were written on the postcard except the date and name of the sender,
blood like a faucet pouring from his mouth—

the day Scarlatti comes into the world
an adventure in mapping swings to court, bus stop to the park,
the cat gliding from pillows to papers on desk—

like the recordings Gershwin made for Columbia in 1926, Gertrude what's-her-name
describes what happened to rhythm—color versus dance
which today spells "archipelago,"
stiletto eyebrows even in the music which by this time sounds metallic—

ice in response to isolation, the pumpkin collapses enroute to compose—
until the mercury hits the arrow, the editorial "we"
is worlds away, assumes nothing—

we now take you to Princeton, where the shovel is tired of all that moves—
it was Thursday morning in a thousand radio places
when I went to build the violin
in the last five minutes of *Twelfth Night*, I confess—

she has played with him since they were two—
now in bed with her arm up
his address indicates "artist," the bear hug takes her breath away—

she stopped in Des Moines to preview the route, turned off half way to Denver—
aa and *pahoehoe* correct as far as terms go, Mozart next
to content, this sentence followed
how the calving of icebergs leaves Pachelbel inaudible—

to think such a system of thought-up sound
he wanted yellow to speak—whence tonality, listen to the rhythm
of the cueball lost in a poolroom somewhere in Iowa—

say it's Brubeck live in '53, the intensity with which he smokes a measure of his intellect
when the sentence takes charge—the chicken's vestigial reptile claw,
the penguin who won't nudge her egg back to nest
until she means to approach the structure of perfect lives—

I never said "chips from a bird's-mouth cut nestled in sawdust"
expecting a miracle but settling for prose,
herons and egrets nesting each spring in a manner most people will not understand—

like a man who leaves behind a trail of weeping women, a loiterer in the vacant wrinkled bed—
I'm sorry you want such memories back, but the multi-colored moth wings
camouflaged on Tiffany's "View of Oyster Bay"
won't be missed in the light the sun turned just before plunging into the sea—

the jet above the plane banking north into a room with no depth of field,
the greatest living poet has been dead for years—
who knows what's going on?—

one who raised a test tube to fate as if the music of West Java wasn't banned,
its coherent system of tuning sound—otherwise ideas
about place, how architectonic
savages will soon be feeding beside the drowned-in-perfume fly—

duet for four hands, rebuttal not allowed—translated from Latin
this reads "don't let the bastards get you down,"
green over black lines visible at fifty paces, Navajo-white trimmed in tropical-birch—

the physics of music best explained as resonance in a hollow box,
meaning if every throat were different each of the chords would be equally complex—
at the same time, suppose this unraveling of her life were to send her Sandro Botticelli for the night,
is it any surprise he does with junk what he used to do as a child?—

the power of prayer whose contents shimmer above the wood-burning stove—
this feeling won them over, specifically the dove on the wall
smudged with pencil that softens the conclusion—

learning to count to zero first, mirror bound to a window facing the neighbors' private lives—
what you made as a child is called nothing, a heavy-lidded sleeper lurching
around curves, wrists scarred where you climbed the cyclone fence
to the Forest of Arden known as Cape Fear, the leaves blown up along the so-called scenic route—

she smiled injecting the virus under his skin, as if he could have governed without her—
like the man who wastes his too too sullied flesh, a script in the path to show us how to read the book,
shrouds over boxes in a glass case driving toward the fugitive beach—

shoulder to shoulder on the carpet of fall, oncoming vehicles need not stop
with patterns that slow down—the camera implies
I therefore am, one being six
times four times six divided by four divided by six, music representing numerical order—

her soft lenses weren't easy to get out, but after four brandies anything seemed possible—
like vox and rabbit in cream, the methods of projective geometry
service from Latin mobile, French mobile—

accurate to the half-inch, he said he hadn't come to criticize the press—
not a breath pushing in front of the front pushing in,
Barbie is pink inside her tin can
constructing a diagram for the groups called "foot," "lead" and "anchor"—

like tripods on Trinidad or hand grenades in Grenada, central heat in China
boxes the leaks which haven't yet been fixed, sound made
by opening the window in the wind—

NINE

Speaking of someone who lives in the most distant of rooms
as if Monk's music were his middle name, Sphere,
picture the square whose bronze canters when the light on the dashboard warns SHIFT,
matches dropping to the sidewalk, sonata framed for prepared piano—

meaning again Battista Sforza, d'Urbino's stare, the more he thinks about whose name
the less it seems to mean "me"—happy the bride the sun shines on
speaking freely of homophones, the voice at the about-to-swing Dutch door—

lilting comes back to want more of the Bach Cantata, thinking that she plans
the vulture on the fence post reviewing frost on greens,
letters smuggled from jail inside a visitor's vagina—sand fairways
characteristic of Persian Gulf golf, along with lizard-hole hazards and brown greens—

garlic suggests a Mediterranean connection, superior Hitchcock given the violins
on the long sleepy drive to Suite 1, 1782, the toll taker's chin
who doesn't know *anything* about shiatzu—

at Fatama and Lourdes the Virgin appears to a young girl, a moment of bright sun followed by hail
followed by the difference between twenty minutes and the champagne
she will open first, the bevelled mirror's *stroke,*
push down, stand up, crank! bone marrow brittle as shells—

walking to breakfast in a bathrobe, her leisure to finish the book—
a sax floats from the blue cliffs,
the oldest cat chomping a bird feathers and all—

under fluorescent lights the smoke looked purpler—such relaxed lines
she read the book in lieu of driving, running the risk of definition changed in 1960
to a metamorphic style in which little rhymed with reason,
thinking Getz had played the last four—

an arrangement in black and white becomes Whistler's mother, affirming the door
to the room light enters, the world's space
as down the leaves and shiplap sides of walls November rains—

someone on a fast who sets a shojii screen around her plate
somewhere between form and function—she appeared in his dream wearing a throwaway robe,
more than terry cloth, less than a shawl, trumpet and continuo suggesting
that Richard's testicles had indeed descended—

chance the principle of order that never stops, it's we who turn away under the glass acoustics
—red translucent eyes, the sense of a blue field, curved white swatch
the Moonlight Sonata plays in the next room—

her perfect O defined by its space "au centre d'un monde de cristal"—
his mind set sotto voce, claustrophobic
in the impossible sense that he threw his arms around me
thinking of triangles poised on the wave of time, France literally in the way—

primer white, no way of knowing what will turn up next
—instead of I Love Lucy You Are There
were it possible to expect the surprise in her arms, the lover's sleeping cat—

the first word of a sentence I dreamed I forgot augments the dominant thirteenth,
for "Blue Moon" go to the non-smoking table with red napkins
which is far away—verbal inevitability
advancing toward Saturday, the blond who answers to Zebra—

at which point counterpoint takes over, each sentence starting from scratch ten spaces
from NO PARKING, typology a means of spanning the abyss the voice
changes as the poem begins—softer, breathless, hushed—

the symbol for square root less a pinch of valerian,
why did the chemist need space to meditate?—self-control impossible
according to reports of a catfish on the Oceola Interstate,
after the movie he tried to go *ahhhhh!*—

what seems to complete the novel merely ends it—
necking in the front seat, being moved to ask *"can* one avoid the rain in Spain?"
if Klimt hangs in the west, O'Keeffe in the east—

her long-neglected mauve hysteria thrusting its way to the railing,
everyone was fooling around with poetry—
I too am committed as long as the weather holds, Steinway
propped open for fuller sound, the grove of level trees stretching to the lemon—

a structure the atoms of the molecule
opens the answer up to the room—subject to the moon within her lies
an endless calendar, what a place to take your life—

its face lifting 3000 feet, she dreamed the garden through the wave's back door,
joined the party dressed to kill—stop what, having a good time
around a scaled-down "children get on board,"
all six corpses with their throats slit, unlisted numbers?—

to decide between angel blush and tango-tango the Old Masters gathered in Delft,
their magnitude at various frequencies indicating yellow—
as for Eiffel's vertiginous stairs, a color the system names could sway—

meaning to say this precisely, you might give the trout more than seven minutes,
thinned flesh-colored paint under bitten nails assuming the film is *Mary Had A Little Lamb*—
meaning to put this *succinctly*, to plant the avocado in the glass
think about tomorrow without alarm—

in what sense is French vanilla better than butter?—strange color, flavor a backward glancing
of violins edged aside by the cellos, in a word the preposition would make
adrenalin poisoning, which may be only the question—

like waves of rhythm on four congas, she was percussive but couldn't keep track of it
slinking her bones against the wall as if no one could see her—the light constant as The Heartbreaks,
Larks, Ravens, Robins, Swallows, Toppers, Syncopators, Striders and Billy
and His Buddies on Doo-Wop Delights tonight—

the notion of motion in music, counterpoint books in any language all the same—
the ants come after syrup spilled on berries under the empty branch, thirty-second bits and pieces
shuffled to find an arrangement the ocean at maximum roars—

morning curbs awash, frogs lifting throats to the wind, what you see is not the same
picture recorded in a voice—folded, the sun would shine on you
I used to think, play when the page turned
regardless of the rose-stuffed couch whose Ur-print looks so faded—

spelling "beguine," "annaxxacanthus," O flightless parrot,
where then moored the ancient skerry?—Hamlet's father's ghost wants his due
and the woman who cuts hay doesn't have it—

the librarian always the first to arrive, her doves in memory of a suicide kept on ice—
Honolulu, Yokohama, Hong Kong, Manila, he too was reading Proust
when the war broke out, whose clothes don't wrinkle
since grandmother dialed with a wand instead of her nails—

Seasons Greetings from a Bedu tent, where the sense of sleeping on the tablecloth appeals to the cat—
the "A" side drives the storm track north to the empty quarter, where you forget
you don't know the chord from the key, in the sense of sleep—

too active to give up surgery, he used to be able to tell a '57 Bel Air
enough to stop him from drinking coffee—now lets a couple of shingles bar the ledge,
talks of the Dalkon Shield whose hoop screwed the sea's concert
"so you can't even shit without meeting a saint"—

after hours of soft curves a redwood splinter—theory at the top of the chart
when another fish blows the wash north by northwest into plumes,
why not learn to read the right way, monosyllabically, fingers tandem inventing the keys—

TEN

On her way to Australia she changed her mind—will the slow curve leave
the shadow train when it looks like it looks like rain?
a unique impression of the sixth
state of the print followed by a ring of bait in the glass lagoon?—

film noir names the angle of a stowaway cruise to the Islands—
skipping lunch after breakfast,
the prospect of leaving makes life look good—

almost opposite Calle Embarcadero, did it ever feel bad to go back to Bach?—
so cold in the kitchen the cats were asleep
dreaming a marvellous hollow armory sound, Shorty Jacobs
the soloist in Stardust, who must have been a night from hitting New York—

nor do I think my father read the Bible eleven inches from the hummingbird's trance—
standing back from the body he would shoot
so the brain wouldn't splat, did he drive down said green valley?—

simply to have said "nor do I think my father read the Bible,"
compare the wall's line to horizon
intercepted by forms shifting to northwest 15 knots—
I say this not to be misconstrued, but the past isn't only ten minutes ago—

a valid driver's license would have allowed Biff to drive a cab
but until it's deleted the line will be vague—
meaning to make myself more remote, I dream the wall and how to get it straight—

on the tennis court or something like it, my brother dressed in knotted beard
attacked on the streets of Berlin for the pin in his cheek
speaking of nihilism, which reminds me
of the time I woke to the bear on my pillow, listening—

moist air converging with arctic mass, writing doesn't have to speak in total silence—
adrenalin runs on the time you turn around to Mozart, seas building
to eighteen feet in the tree the cat calls home—

supposing she's the best dressed woman in town, runs a draw down which even deer won't follow—
blowing kids in fields away with a countergirl's obligatory "Hello,"
how is Garbo reminiscent of Rameau
losing the list jammed in his breast pocket filled with scars?—

the two dogs never alike, unlike chrysanthemums, two motets wrapped in a stuffed corpse
which doesn't help to explain why phone calls don't get along with wool—
the eye who calls the shutter back to Renaissance warmth—

like Rembrandt/Goya, Diebenkorn/de Kooning, this line crossed out results in static—
consider the paintings of Miro at ninety upside down, scissors on a desk
now cutting the dahlias' stems aslant, how her hem shows
when the conversation slips to "I'm dating a man with a Lear jet, wish me luck"—

pants should break above the shoe, the so-called Edwardian cuff
including the dryer that shrinks a lace spread—when he hears her slippers leave the room
the camera zooms to ducks in a row, the amber-eyed cat who stares down stars—

filmed the second time slower, never quite developing those cat-like pirouettes
so glassy-eyed around the lagoon, the same soup on the stove
as before the henna receiver missing an ear,
violins wrapped in a small town in Vermont—am I obsessive-compulsive to be going this far?—

and what do you remember about 24 September?—the twins liked the faster songs,
each in the style of a different master, her head
in a series of facing mirrors like paper the water leaves curled—

in all seven works the orange looks bright, its superimposed logics of "sweet is"
running to "is sweet," whose signature occurs in either corner—
a comma whether syntax demands it or not,
conflict as large as the person who means to say "understand" not "under stand"—

how everything changed seeing Elvis in person—Marpessa Dawn
in Stuyvesant Town, the line between points spiraling toward nerves, not noise,
wherein lies the music's meaning, its clear blue cold conclusion—

pairs matched according to this sense of pace, a tropical landscape
like the browns in a tale of West Yellowstone trout—
now the trees "persimmon," "mahogany," no skies ten feet off the ground
untitled because of the nothing in it, the women over and over again in a building cheap as dirt—

within the hour they began to fool around, not that he got robbed exactly—
Miss Zena Dares dead? a two-step down her lover's vein,
the couple becoming more like one another until the book, calm and placid on the surface—

the two Kens between the Barbies almost dry—eggshell cracked,
mute as is, the woman at the window with a bowl
whose eyes as I moved past followed, all the milk white blue in the world
standing the sort of change one minds to make hours from zero—

orchid, French windows, pittosporum, the neighbor's roof's horizon—call it the sort of cold
wet penetrates, reproduction a range of tones
possibly recording my name, the cat crawling under the down quilt—

after a point talk won't help—company town, zinc involved in trying to set the music to the words
the blue ice crystal airs, a sense of vertigo
six or eight times later objectively defined as "background"
standing in the corner happy again, ears plugged, words as if life depended—

mud like the "k" in knife, silent, house lights dim but then what?—
he touched her shoulder, meaning they were to leave the city filmed as it was,
close-up of eyes gone red where the road narrowed—

photowipe speck behind the lens, she threatened to serve him faux French cuisine,
nor was it fair to say his treatment of her was deep throat
although the words themselves were not untrue—do you get the feeling
all he wrote was a charade, or think your teacher would whistle at plays in a beret?—

does the reader need to know this in order to read the book?—
who would think you framed the bridge at Arles?—
you don't taste the flea's blood in mine?—

on the way to the Bronx mine is the only blond head in sight—a small concept of structure
on top of what seems a chaos of events, I probably exaggerate
to say the wave was five feet, formal logic
in the corner of the garage where the savage prepares to wring her gorgeous white neck—

so Copland are those lofty decrescendos—like others he too died of cancer
no matter what the bridge called HUGE SURF
POUNDS COAST, the cat losing weight at an alarming rate—

smoke in the blue light of the driveway, what does love have to do with gospel?—
think of the typical London flat, hole-in-the-wall, Nottinghill Gate,
the figs overcome with brandied syrup, the roses in her hair
when he refused to cut back on his overtime, his wife suggesting divorce—

nothing loves the pine's acid like its needles—his bad day carried on and on,
the cold mounting feet first, Mozart instead of talk
after the two-martini dinner, the jew's-harpist's cracked tooth—

music at the speed of sound, the piece provoked a consternation rarely seen in the concert hall—
the usual geriatric crowd was there, white-haired, well-dressed,
hardly explosive, cars in head lights
whizzing past what words would do (asteroid slash dinosaur)—

pronoun for which there is no substitute, a sea of rising voices downstairs
—yes, John has delved quite a bit into the mysteries
of the French approach to language, a shining light in the hedge that leaves me speechless—

ELEVEN

Absorbed in *The Murder of Representation in Literature*, with what herbs did they spike your sleep?—
when I lie down on the stones it starts to rain, *Heidi*
slipping into the third person like a rabbit skinned in the butcher's window,
his wife or her father hacked to pieces by the beach?—

she meant it when she said he could share her bed "anytime"—
at the risk of sounding lit, the fire warmed the room, the Sphinx was growing his beard
with four pairs of feet clad in fur slippers, the mock apple shaplier pruned—

anonymous dances when the fire burns low,
it's odd we never met in what Bill Berkson calls Celesteville—
roll over, dream a little longer,
glass where shattered an overturned wreck, the forest barely stacked against the cold—

sound objects to the extent that chance determines rote, give me local habitation and a name—
the women still washed clothes at the well, "I have a dog"
meaning a dog comes to my house, Franco-Prussian or Russo-Japanese will do—

when the kitchen breaks into French the cats will eat, "c'est vraiment un paradis ici"—
she was waiting for something, what was the point?
then had a dream she would ask "where will I live my life next?"
—there was no one in the cafe but a beautiful boy, and he said "come with me"—

instead of a walk the dog walks me—now and then a year from now mistakes are possible,
Ives as in Charles trimming the hedge, the rabbit better the second day,
the "it" in "about" whose audience believes is tragic—

watching the road in time rhythm defines as tone,
arhythmic something one doesn't mind—
theme starts at the end of variation, suicide by hanging,
the Arabian pulled at the vet check lame, clocks that silence light as a leaf—

descending the mountain note the sun intenser at every turn—she cried and cried
herself to sleep, arcade deserted
at the level of the phrase, Gieseking without the pedal—

the cat left a deal in the cosmic scheme—quiver shutter, Polaroid flex,
the mouthpiece added "to be able to be blown" in quarter and three-quarter note tones
—circle outside the ring still listening,
positions taken, haunches locked, how soon the world becomes historic—

in Gaelic the odd ways of "to be in my shape"—they acquired a taste for running amok,
family billed for the bullet that shoots their father, brother, son
in the heart of the sperm whale's food chain—

wrapped in a room inside a room, the kimono keeps her warm
printed upside down—half a turn sign missing, labial meaning heart on a cuff,
a discontinuous modality of real sometime duo pianists
taste starts at the end of the bus—

having taken vows of silence, now I'm fully awake—the title means nothing
but its pretty name, eucalyptus rounds on the slope not cows, bird whistles about to jump start
all I think to feel in the rising sound of knuckle, bone at noon—

the birth of two voices in relation of three to five—another story
player unexpectedly piano
in bed with Billie Holiday, if he didn't get some sleep he'd die
after imagined radio blank, island impossible—

her letter stopped on the word "clock," Mozart's birthday almost done—
it had to have been someone's fault, the chemist's wife discovering mussels in Brussels, sex at home
no hands could play so humanly fast, sometimes up to a year to complete five minutes—

Nick used to be smarter than his older brother until his brain got smashed
driving to Fresno—the other stories were all in my real voice,
everyone wanting to write *Tess of the d'Urbervilles* set in old New Mexico,
who else could use the word "pachuco" so well?—

slowly the desk unclutters itself—that I believe was a pipe organ
the dog sighs in a few barks, the future anticipated in the form of an absolute danger
as the tape loops forth "borrow my pillow, the text has a face"—

"watch for black 'n white skunks 'n heifers"—she went back to her language
while I stayed in mine, halls exhausting as a field of light,
redwood waltzing east above Texas plates,
the flowered couch with a coffee in the other twitching hand—

who does he think the prince was, from which planet
boxes round which the yard plants—I'll talk to you later absolutely
asks the cat who would share my chair—

say things are grim, perhaps embarrassing, horses in the field fucking in the fog,
you too can vacation in Vegas—another Hungarian, Bartok
played a piano in his home as a child,
ream awl/holding saw/dowel threader/auger bit/spoke shave/bitstock—

Paris the seasoned traveler often likened to Genève
brushes hues in red, color map of the world—returning the glass surface
the glare would out, the cello carries the far guitar—

last on her list of sunspots, her fingerprints when she leaves the church
faster than the middle voice surrounding two doubling to four,
later eight, aggregates to follow—he loves to look
when she tumbles into bed without a bath, gets up at three to draw one—

the sidewalks in South China even more than crowded,
the rooms in Tangier five flights up—
broil the quail with bacon toothpicked to its delicate wing-white breast—

the Scotch Tape method a matter of layers
followed by predictions, the scene changes from a walk to the train
to Shakespeare & Company left by the tub—
proving hard boiled, she fingered the catsup from a styrofoam box—

the second "what" sharp, half beat, moves once where once you moved—
his word for language wasn't quite sophisticated
wanting to count the comma-shaped band of clouds from satellite space—

rhyming terms with her, for clattered pages search the score—
de Kooning broke the ice, nine months on a wall
widening the field, runoff wearing away at rake or ridge when there is one,
nails spotted down the line committed to work—

Scarlatti's Kirkpatrick, Mozart's K—she nods when he calls the song a poem
whoever wrote the music, says "this is an ultrasound test"
mossed in senses on the verge of out—

reading today he was middle aged, and she wasn't even squatting—at the last minute
in a violet dress, Tahiti-baby-red the least expressed amount of color
or end of color, ice blue eyes when he leaves Atlanta
listening to the same signals groping toward Gropius, unable to recall—

yes, you do suffer the grand disappointments, index finger bending the white pen, Lebanon
anon become the problem—fed the dogs would lap sleep, "chateaux"
fathom the sound of Betty Carter's breath—

come in Mission Specialist Surgeon, over—his background included work in aesthetics,
meaning in music the chair is a perfect place to sleep or go upstairs
to another picture—something the rain blooms
like content, after which nothing need be said but in closing found—

as the notes spread out from F-sharp, Burt Lancaster lights his third Italian-made cigar,
catches the late flight home from Hilo, will call tomorrow—
pink and ochre present the obvious challenge, spring the hinge won't snap—

TWELVE

Stones lichen-laced in the dew-green field the ultimate shock—film for example
the afterimage you leave, the anvil edge of prairie spring
—she wrapped around him the dance
of the seven veils, but he would have none of it, no sale—

lights dimmed before the clap of thunder, I mean the real spring—
books on the front seat including Husserl and Kant
dismantle the painting, get rid of lines more pleasing than ears had ever heard—

from now on let the record be The Spiders, the tones heard before fade—
in the west clouds *could* mean rain
picking up the words the pencil found, LEFT TURN
in U.S. intelligence, a burning tanker sinks the Straights of Hormuz—

picture Big Nurse on the cover of her second book of hospital tales, gauze in mouth
coming out bloodstained, surgical sleep next door to death—
knowing you had hit the wrong note, note what you did was improvise—

"obsolete" was a telephone word meaning sidestepping puddles,
swallows building mud under eaves, a blister where the handle kissed my palm—
in astronomical terms, who's the bird the bird watcher watches,
McCartney soaring a fifth on "yes she's falling"?—

speakers in the next room a little back from Bach, Roman blinds the full-on lunar spectacle—
perhaps the wake did him good, the pruned plum's mate blossom wild,
extra kindling notwithstanding she had a match—

in a letter as of surprise the ruse was also the lesson—the door key hidden above the door
colored by delux, the coda aired for all to breathe the death of words
the compass forgot, the low tones dogs don't hear
raining something inside and out, the object you wanted writing holes—

clouds after clearing, Mozart's Divertimento ahead of its time—suicide reminds us
a little of nobody, the scale of glass in a tanned foot
heavenly green, earthly green caressing the patch across the ditch—

being pregnant, Katie longed for the sensation of leaning down in the frozen peas
—photo lichens on graphic rock, bone-loss merely mise-en-scène,
"all hands for the hawser!" as we made fast
where lo, the lights of Los Angeles shone before us, and we were sore amazed—

silver stamped to koto music his work slowed, her emphysemic father wintered in Naples—
I too have always wanted to plié "A Train," practice limited to the window
closed on vulnerability, Rubens' advancing heightening white—

after the shower she stands by the mirror sucking her thumb—hair ideal but the twist is lost,
aluminum read like a screen one can't see the side of, doves or something
the high point of my nap, embellishments borrowed
from the preceding presenting the beat taste of pellucid speech—

"how may people here share a deep commitment to nothing?"—not the husband
but a Japanese friend in the book *The Victimized Woman*,
the shutter tripped once before ready—

she begins with the principle note, trilling amidst the tawdry door
as movement throughout the work in varied cadences once pronounced "herbs" with an "h"—
gardens the time the surface strokes, tonic for those who complain
of the near past clarity of spatial systems—

the camera "looks up" its subject, the words pasted
together striking with beautiful proportion—Mohican flecks,
yellow-aqua, chapter headings read—

though 2004 is a leap year, the attack will be led by children and mullahs—switching channels
the freedom of total control, grammar mistakes a test of where the scissors go,
Noah Webster's story real as a method for arranging holes
in New Hampshire, the facts themselves buried in tracks to the Pole—

Gropius speaks the glass text constructed of a thousand hands, the card punched South Pacific
left as jasper, clear as stone—consider World's Fairs on the words "orbit,"
"circulation of traffic demands the straight line"—

"the sentence bound as color field watches the seconds not spin"
at twelve to five, the place of stones
which wasn't said to the future—falling bodies taken to light,
how the young man trapped in an armchair looks at the crowd, takes the drop with the lip—

notes exploring a range of frequencies possible within a system whose limits cannot be fixed—
target the room and all therein besides the window smashed,
who knows how the scrap projects a peak, begins the Swan Lake pas de deux—

the principle dancer stepping ahead of the pack, as if to reflect upon how when a person
gets a cab it's his cab, as whitewash lets the cedar show, canvas blinds—
the owners of the house had made it big in margarine,
the pilgrims sauntered to the Holy Land, looked around, booked return passage to L.A.—

to invent volcanoes, etc. in the name of science, azure clear to the stratosphere,
she drops a name just to get even—palm of blisters, mind of milk
ties the sarong around her breasts (Nth is for now)—

jet after jet leaves the ground, but like Charles Ives "X" is hardly known—
the dentist fills his mouth with plaster, the stranger in the bar who knows your friend
tends to confuse him with none of the above, Trotsky most upset
his fellow Ukrainians can't buy bread—

you can always write *something* on the ballot, comrade—"William Randolph Hearst"
called a rain of tears, a cloud of dark disdain, earth moving
the hillside after it slips, conjugal visit topics restricted to dogs and kids—

meaning vivid as technicolor, don't raise your voice "don't raise *your* voice"—
no, I haven't been in a movie, nor was Ophelia
strewing flowers, excited as the reader becoming what book
by what means no longer present, Hillary changing his cashmere blazer—

doing the floor plan measure the walls, she wants her shoes beside the bed—
I too love my PIT BULL,
under her shirt her undershirt holding my breath—

the poem appears years after sale of a ticket at the same price (illustration),
horses found with their legs tied, splayed—
"play" with ferns bending, my part beyond the moment turned inward,
"don't maul me" she warned, pulling down her sweater, "no wonder The Cardinals didn't make it"—

asked if ice is a ring around the sun, not to read
in less than 30 seconds sea changes, wistaria pods, stores in the palapa,
a telephone the pigeons bred to be or not erratic—

going back and forth at will, compare text under "juicy," "aromatic," "mid-tone base,"
"conscience," "catechize," "phosphorescent," "licorice"—
she needed the year in pictures to memorize the story up to here,
the amber lens one's best disguise, pronoun the enigma spelled "his" for "mine"—

Chinese notes the yellow page, shapes in the water I dreamed of waking—
avoiding downtown Sunday was a relative thing, the way one's voice pitch changed "parenthesis"
or better still "ear" two minutes after a take, saxophone nodding the moss-grown tongue—

anonymous tarantellas, do salmon bite in the rain?—in two dimensions we understand three,
in the series 1, 3, 4, 7, 11, blank, "blank" is what aesthetic distance
upstairs down the hall around the corner,
the next measure meaning birds, notes that question moves that kill—

blink the vines cover the house, these sounds the difference
between a year in a line one had almost forgotten and the record that's almost done—
monotones, wet paint, contact prints—

Stephen Ratcliffe was born in Boston in 1948 and grew up in the San Francisco Bay Area. His books include *Campion: On Song, [where late the sweet] BIRDS SANG, spaces in the light said to be where one/ comes from* and *Selected Letters*. He is editor and publisher of Avenue B. He lives in Bolinas, California and teaches at Mills College in Oakland.

The Figures

Michael Anderson/Melanie Neilson *Tripled Sixes/Prop and Guide* $5.00
Bruce Andrews *Tizzy Boost* $10.00
Rae Armantrout *Extremities* $5.00
David Benedetti *Nictitating Membrane* $5.00
Steve Benson *Blue Book* $12.50
Alan Bernheimer *Cafe Isotope* $7.50
John Brandi *Diary from a Journey to the Middle of the World* $9.00
Summer Brenner *From the Heart to the Center* $7.50
Summer Brenner *The Soft Room* $7.50
David Bromige *My Poetry* $10.00
Laura Chester *My Pleasure* $10.00
Laura Chester *Watermark* $10.00
Tom Clark *Baseball* $10.00
Clark Coolidge *For Kurt Cobain* $5.00
Clark Coolidge *At Egypt* $7.50
Clark Coolidge *The Book of During* $15.00
Clark Coolidge *The Crystal Text* $10.00
Clark Coolidge *Melencolia* $5.00
Clark Coolidge *Mine: The One That Enters the Stories* $10.00
Clark Coolidge *Odes of Roba* $12.00
Clark Coolidge & Larry Fagin *On the Pumice of Morons* $5.00
William Corbett *Remembrances* $5.00
Michael Davidson *Analogy of the Ion* $5.00
Lydia Davis *Story and Other Stories* $10.00
Christopher Dewdney *Concordat Proviso Ascendant* $7.50
Johanna Drucker *Italy* $6.00
Kenward Elmslie & Joe Brainard *The Champ* $12.00
Norman Fischer *On Whether or Not to Believe in Your Mind* $7.50
Kathleen Fraser *Each Next* $7.50
Michael Friedman *Cameo* *$5.00*
Gloria Frym *Back to Forth* $7.50
Merrill Gilfillan *River Through Rivertown* $7.50
Michael Gizzi *Just Like A Real Italian Kid* $5.00
Michael Gizzi *A Jar in Bedlam* $5.00
John Godfrey *Midnight On Your Left* $7.50
Michael Gottlieb *New York* $10.00
Lyn Hejinian *Oxota: A Short Russian Novel* $15.00
Paul Hoover *Idea* $10.00
Fanny Howe *Introduction to the World* $7.50

Bill Luoma *My Trip to New York City* $5.00
Musa McKim *Alone With The Moon* $12.00
Melanie Neilson/Michael Anderson *Prop and Guide/Tripled Sixes* $5.00
Ron Padgett *Ted* $10.00
Ron Padgett *The Big Something* $7.50
Ron Padgett & Clark Coolidge *Supernatural Overtones* $7.50
Bob Perelman *Captive Audience* $7.50
Bob Perelman *a.k.a.* $10.00
Bob Perelman *The First World* $7.50
Stephen Ratcliffe *Present Tense* $12.00
Tom Raworth *Tottering State* $11.50
Tom Raworth *Emptily* $5.00
Tom Raworth *The Vein* $4.00
Kit Robinson *Down and Back* $7.50
Kit Robinson *Covers* $4.00
Stephen Rodefer *Four Lectures* $10.00
Stephen Rodefer *Emergency Measures* $7.50
Peter Schjeldahl *Columns and Catalogues* $15.00
Peter Schjeldahl *The 7 Days Art Columns* $12.50
Ron Silliman *Tjanting* $10.00
Ron Silliman *What* $10.00
Julia Vose *Moved Out on the Inside* $10.00
Guy Williams *Selected Works 1976-1982,* essay by Gus Blaisdell $10.00
Geoffrey Young *Rocks and Deals* $5.00
Geoffrey Young *Subject to Fits* $10.00